CW00509561

exeter & devon arts centre
EXETER POETRY PRIZE
1998

ANTHOLOGY
Selected by Lawrence Sail

ODYSSEY PRESS

ODYSSEY PRESS
Coleridge Cottage
Nether Stowey
Somerset

in association with
EXETER & DEVON ARTS CENTRE
Bradninch Place
Gandy Street
Exeter
Devon

© 1998

ISBN 1 897654 48 0

CONTENTS

FOREWORD

We are once again delighted to bring you an Anthology of poems, for 1998 chosen by Lawrence Sail, from submissions to The Exeter Poetry Prize.

The poems here come from what was the largest entry in the four years that the Prize has been organised by *Exeter & Devon Arts Centre*, and our congratulations go to those included here, with thanks to those who contributed to the success of this project.

I believe it gives a small insight into the picture of the diversity of people writing poetry today, and I hope it helps inform the way our ongoing literature programme at the Arts Centre can develop to be meaningful to both readers and writers.

Andy Morley
Exeter & Devon Arts Centre

JUDGE'S REPORT

This year's competition attracted close on 2,500 poems covering a wide range of subjects. The most popular theme was one of poetry's oldest, the business of love – requited, unrequited, often viewed in its aftermath, and sometimes seen in the context of family or of elegy. Not far behind in number were poems focusing on the seasons (autumn more than the other three), weather or landscape. The passage of time, with its corollary of human ageing, accounted for another distinct group, as did poems set in Devon, Cornwall or elsewhere in the south west, some of them written in local dialect. In contrast, there were also poems of travel and place which between them went from Bosnia to Bukaru to Beijing, amongst many other locations. There were poems in praise of animals (a clear preference here for cats), as well as a deal of light and comic verse. And, though fewer in number than I had anticipated, there were poems of occasion – the death of Princess Diana, the Millennium, Hale Bopp.

Formally, the entries offered a similar variety. Alongside verse of assorted degrees of freedom, there were sonnets, villanelles, sestinas, blank verse, even an acrostic whose initial letters were a lament for the untimely death of the poet Frances Horovitz. But easily the most striking feature was the widespread use of full rhyme: too often, it must be said, deployed with little enough regard for the mood or intention of the poem, or for natural word order and diction. Others writers relied on the straightforward expression of strongly held views or emotions, without much concern for technique or memorability: but sincerity alone cannot guarantee a successful poem. Nor can the use of language once considered poetic in a high-flown style, but now archaic and lifeless. It is depressing to find this mode still being used, not least because it suggests that the writer is not a reader, at least not of contemporary poems, and so lacks any awareness of what techniques and possibilities are currently available.

However, the impressive standard of the best poems was brought home to me emphatically by the difficulties of my task; first, in narrowing my selection to the poems for inclusion in this anthology; then, in compiling a short list; and finally, in choosing the prize winners. On the way I found much to enjoy. There were a number of poems which were really striking in part, while not overall quite living up to their best moments: but some of these were so good that I lamented their exclusion. And when it came to the final stages I had the pleasures of, for instance, John Whitworth's zestful, *DOCTOR DOUBLEGOER'S PRESCRIPTIONS,* Mimi Khalvati's thoughtful *LIFE IN ART,* the vividness of *COOKING FISH* by Sue Hubbard, and the exact evocation of Matthew Barton's *H. M. PLUTO'S MEN.*

The winner of the first prize is **Greta Stoddart** for her poem *THREE MEN IN A BOAT,* which I found memorable at the outset and which became more so as I got to know it better. I admire the clarity and verve of its narrative, but also the undertones and the individuality of outlook which came through with increasing weight on re-reading. My admiration did, though, have to come to terms with the poem's title. *FAR PLACES* by **Sheenagh Pugh,** which wins the second prize is beautifully poised. Notable for its skilful use of rhyme and near-rhyme, the poem sustains its sense of a quest and rounds to a most satisfying, if wistful, conclusion. The third prize goes to **John Mole** for *THE PROMISE,* a subtle and, I find, moving poem. Not only does it give the reader work to do, but its recreation of an Edenic heartland and the way in which the poem progresses, with the eerie seamlessness of a true dream, are real accomplishments. Quite different, but equally memorable in its way, is *NIGHTSHELTER DEC. TWENTYFIVE* by **Terry Pritchard**, winner of the supplementary prize, for a poet based in Exeter. Here is evidence of an acute ear for speech patterns, a mind quick to make associations, and a real enjoyment of language.

I hope that readers of the anthology will derive as much pleasure from the poems as I have.

Lawrence Sail

Greta Stoddart
THREE MEN IN A BOAT

And me. Miles out, bobbing. Thinking of fish.
Isn't it stickleback who go from red to green
then back again when they mate? Or when they die?

The rods lean off, bending to the tug of the ocean.
No one knows. Only the waves that pop and slurp,
the empty bucket at our feet, knocking then –

like a gust from nowhere, he jerks up and *Yee-ha!*
swings his rod above our heads in a wild arc.
The boat wobbles and –

I hardly feel the hook catch my throat, a graze
like the wing of something light, but then I know,
                                                             sense
the heart gently quicken, slow plunge of blood.

And the thing that first gripped me when I lay in a
                                        school field
under a black, galactic sky, the very thing
that could cause a fork to freeze, mid-air, at a dinner

was coming to me now as I sat, hooked, in front of
                                        the horizon,
seeing the little lights coming on, steady
                                        and shivering,
the great white shell of sky, a tanker stock-still.

The men, red-faced, fussed with knives and engines,
their fingers thick around my throat as I sat and felt
every nerve, every muscle and every limb.

fall, perfect, like the simple fate of silk landing,
into place. And there, the one in the white shirt –
how odd! One with whom I was simply glad to spend

the nights should be with me now, the very moment
                                        I become
extinct; his face, so grim, so concerned, so human,
                                        the last
I see. *There's the bastard!* A voice from
                                        another world,

a slap on the back, peck on the cheek, the
                                        engine steps up
its whine and before I know it we're at the
                                        bar, knocking
back the beers, taking turns to tell our story
to the locals in our bad, our broken, Spanish.

SECOND PRIZE WINNER

Sheenagh Pugh
FAR PLACES

So he made it, in the end, to the top
of the west ridge; half an hour longer
by the track, while his sons went straight up
and waited for him, lounging on the heather,

laughing. He saw the mica in the rock
once more, flashing silver in the sun,
and thought, as he paused to get his breath back,
I couldn't stand not seeing it again.

And then the haul, over miles of hill
and moorland, stumbling in and out
of peat cuttings, watching his footing, while
they strode so far ahead, he couldn't shout

to them. Out of sight. He knew he'd find them
where he had led them all those years ago;
by the steep waterfall. They'd wait for him,
watching the water mist and cream and rainbow,

as mesmerised as ever. He'd rest a minute,
then scramble down beside them in the spray,
or maybe not: the view from the green height
was good enough for most folks. Either way,

it would be worth the walk, the tiredness,
to look again and feel it stop his heart.
But every distant, high, uncommon place
is getting further, harder: more effort

13

for the same prize. *One day,* the thought nags,
you'll say no. Not got the lungs: too stiff.
Or it won't be the breath, the back, the legs,
but the will. And his throat clamps with grief

for the far places: snapshots in a frame,
dim memories; a shard of silver rock
turned in the hand. The glint isn't the same
out of the sun; you never get it back.

John Mole
THE PROMISE

After five months
I meet her in a dream
with all the pain forgotten,
with the swelling in her legs
gone down, just back
from driving into town
and laden happily
with groceries. She says
Let's see about them later
as we run together
out into the garden as it was
in the beginning, where
an empty seat still swinging
waits on my father's lawn,
unrusted, primal
in its lick of emerald paint,
then there she sits again
before I know it, laughing,
Push me, push me, harder,
oh if he could see us
but we'll tell him won't we
when we get there?
with her young, just-married face
alight in expectation, and myself
once more the child seized suddenly
and held tight on her lap
until whichever of us wakes
before the other,
finds him waiting there
and keeps the promise
trusted to a dream.

15

THE EXPRESS & ECHO AWARD

Terry Pritchard
NIGHTSHELTER DEC. TWENTYFIVE

The present
       and other useful items:
paper saucepans and chocolate swords.
Monogrammed donations of course,
Right Honourable this Noble Lord that ...
    Today's soup dragon sheathes the ladle,
plucks a glittering blade
from where it lies on a wipetop table.
    Carves a turkey like a bread boat
as big as Bernard Matthews.
O.K. for veggies then, she croaks
       and other useful items:
duffel coats, indestructible socks,
pocket shaped flat bottled whiskey
fleshed out with the dunnage of usable stock.
    Off to Herzegovina or somewhere similar
bobbed up furious on a brave new map.

The past
       and other useful items:
the turbary of rag picking and old sticks
the pannage of bottles and bones,
    the odd rare worthless place
we could call home
       and other useful items:
half bricks lobbed at a distant fire,
a good kicking in a back alley.
    Breezeblocks from a motorway bridge,
distanced as a smartbomb
nothing touchy feely,
they'd say, ho hum, better them than each other
because, well ...
       they're all good boys really.

The future
       shorter, but still thinking of useful items:
tomorrow's uncertain service resumed,
the occasional wild haired woman
    and all those breaking men,
coughing round the smudge pots
        in a brotherhood of phlegm.

Dickon Abbott
LIFELINE
for Hazel

Like a water-birth, I release my foetal clench
in a duck-dive, spreading to a Hockney splash.
The guideline spills its ink on the pool floor.
My stroke is slower than yours. I inch
along the lane, letting the water wash
my stress away, hands cupped like moles' paws
digging liquid. Time is different here
– fluid, constant, free of the rhythmic tread
of tired soles. As I count each length, I swim
a year of my life. Through the goggles' smear
memories flicker among the bobbing heads.
One of them's yours, butting the surface to win
our lunchtime race. I search for your smile.
Will you still need me, feed me, when I swim a mile?

Pauline Suett Barbieri

HOW CAN I DO A TANGO
WHEN I WAS BROUGHT UP ON ROCK AND ROLL

My floor's well polished,
ready to explore
the brilliantined night.

Line, wind yourself
around my neglected waist,
curve my elbows
into the Tango's flight.
Follow the form
of a Latin lover's plight.

Adjectives flap against
the olive of your skin.
Similes cling to the peaches
and cream of mine.

I bend, love's contortionist,
oiled by WB40
and the smell of the Oleander
in your top suit pocket.

The band scrapes
the notes off the satinized floor.
Lifts them high enough
for us to seize
and push into the space
between our hearts.

I lean into the night,
squeezing
your accordioned presence.
We writhe through
the mirrored ballroom
of our minds,

chase dreams
wedged
in highly polished shoes.

Matthew Barton
H. M. PLUTO'S MEN

OK then, who's fetching the body
at three o'clock?

– for a second I see
the mortuary slab

before I get it – guard-slang
that knocks a man's breathing

body back to so many stones,
pounds, pence

of burden, inconvenience.
And suddenly those hearty, grim

men from childhood stand again:
sweating as they shoulder

grime-shiny bags and reel
on their heels for half a drunk

second to steady
the load, then find

their feet again and quick
step to feed

a black mouth with slurrying
knuckle-bones of coal, the sacks

like skins going flat on their backs.

Chris Beckett
A VOICE SINGING

Try as he might,
the voice would not be kept
inside the house. It was rich
and deep, and Russian as rough vodka.
There was in it
the secret of invisibility,
a presence that was
slippery as sleep,
untrappable as
scent.

Try as he might,
he could not keep
the voice inside. His neighbours
started to complain,
even when he thought the voice
had stopped. And any door
or window, left ajar,
was treated as an invitation
to explore!

Try as he might,
the voice would not be kept
at all. It threatened constantly
to leave and not return.
It seemed to revel in
the mystery of sound,
so close it could
be just inside
the ear.

Oh yes, he tried to follow
where the voice went,
but the house kept him
inside.

Valerie Bridge
HADERSFELD, WINTER, 1950

It seemed the hammering continued all night,
muffled in dreams. Grandmother woke us,
cracking sticks, feeding the fire;
water, locked in,
hissed on the stove.

Feeling the change in light,
we fastened our boots on the verandah,
breathing ice, opening the door:
snow hesitated over the ledge,
fell at our feet.

Out there, the garden white on white,
the sledge shone like Christmas.
Grandmother was whispering,
we could not hold back; stepped outside,
took hold of the sledge.

In that quiet, it tossed on the rope.
We paused, seeing the pump wrapped in its bandages,
then edged through the gate to a land white as
                                    dreams.
Grandmother was urging us laughing uphill;
we ate air until frost burnt our tongues.

It seemed the sledging continued in daylight
brighter than dreams. On the last run,
flying downhill, dusk calling us home,
rocking our sledge, we fell,
arms catching at stars.

Timothy Cassidy
THE KILL

It was a dark day
in September

when we went down
to the hut.

As if they knew
the man said.

They scattered
as he spoke,

flapped their wings
like pistons starting,

bounced off
slatted walls,

choired amok.
We picked one up

and took it out,
plump eucharist

unsoothed
by his sweet mutters.

The axe no sooner hit,
the head fell off

and the yard hosed red
with the body's yell

as it backflipped
on the cobble

to the music
of its throat,

a gymnast
with a long, red veil;

till the legs twitched upright,
clutching air

like a child
in its first bad dream,

the feathers
clinging.

ROAD BUILDING IN INDIA

We will need the bicycle lane, the walking lane
and the cart-pulled-by-a-man lane.
The motorised-rickshaw lane
and the bicycle-rickshaw lane
and one more for the car.

Open lorries, covered lorries and Vespas
will need a lane each.
A lane for buses would help.
Attended animal herds of buffaloes
sheep and goats need a wide lane,
as do decorated elephants.

A small slip road could be provided
for unattended animals such as
monkeys, peacocks, dogs,
the holy cows, camels and pigs.
Bears and their trainers can stand
on the central dividing island.

Along the side of this road,
Jain nuns can walk barefooted
in small groups and push wheelchairs.
Surely the land mass of India
is large enough for such a road.

Andrew Dilger
PARROT

Each day you look as if you'll die:
a thick black tongue
and bloodshot eye, an ember.
Do you even know you're green?

Your laugh is my imagination,
I cough, you do too. Hello, adieu.
I say *Truth* and *Beauty,* you hear *Cuttlefish;*
you squawk, I hear my name.

I smile, you cock your head
as if you understand. As if, as if.
I understand your beak is a hooked hand
that hauls you up and down the cage.

I understand you stretch your wings –
forgotten, battered, antique fans
and run through your four vowels.
And this is gratitude.

And these are walnuts
wedged between the bars,
and we are the same age.
And this is a coincidence.

I come back late –
you wake and bristle,
whistle for the light.
I pass between the furniture like air

and out the other door,
ignore your disembodied call.
And this is natural,
you are an animal.

David Duncombe
JOY RIDER

He likes to ride the roads at night,
burning the high octane of aloneness
in those pure, uncrowded hours, stolen
away from roofs and doors and walls,
to streamline his dreams through the single,
searching beam of the motorcycle.

He likes to genuflect on tree-dark bends
in country lanes, to circle floodlit
roundabouts like a pope on two wheels,
then roll out of a slip road rejoicing,
to celebrate at speed the infinite straights
and merciful curves of the motorway.

He quick-swerves past *a* to *b* traffic:
lorries, rumbling empty or grumbling full,
cars carrying airline people, their minds
on tomorrow, bodies in yesterday,
or a long-distance lover, clocking
the miles to see *'How far would I travel?'*

But before the full-throttled roar settles
to a steady hum, he abandons
the motorway at no particular junction,
leaving it as if he'd not been there,
turning back to minor roads,
headlight hosing away the darkness.

It isn't the stutter and rush of mapped
and programmed trips to *b* or *c*, stages
on the looming route to *z;* his joy
is the flow of a constant, random journey,
the loneliness of passing and passing,
not stopping long enough to disappoint.

Philip Dunn
AT MY NATWEST CASH POINT

I'm not quite there at my NatWest cash point.
A sure sign was the twenty that I left,
Another time, the card. It surely takes
A special kind of absence to do that.

Stood by the kerb, I think what opposites
They are, our soft flesh and motorcars:
How bone must succumb to the engine's mass;
And how embarrassing one's death might be.
And thoughts about clean underpants arise.
But now's not the time to get knocked down:

The universal laws might do their worst,
And if my skull was split and gaping wide
No-one would see the vistas nurtured there:
The rivers coming out of Eden, cool
Climates stacking cumulus over Ur,
And libraries from Uruk brought through Kish
To Nineveh, its palace of the texts,
To Assurbanipal, the World's King,
Where Gilgamesh went walkabout two thousand years.

I would relate it all, like one come out
Of the desert, but keep it to myself.

Edna Eglinton
WHAT GOES UP –

This week it's the lift
that threatens a breakdown.
These smart automatics
don't have the stamina
of the old-time sort
that worked by manpower.

In my junior tea-girl days
of brimming prospects,
soaring hopes,
I delivered urgent letters
to clients in an ancient
building with a sturdy lift.

The liftman stood
within his iron-barred cage,
stripped to the waist.
He flexed the muscles
of his sunbrowned chest
and with a casual grip
upon the naked rope
would hurl me skywards,
with a condescending smile.

The fluttering of my heart
today is indecision.
This neurotic box may fail
while others struggle up
the spiralling stairs.
Rumours gallop faster
than hopeful joggers,
all are threatened.
No-one dares ignore
the counterbalance
always rattling down.

Charles Evans
THE ENDYMION

The Endymion, Introduction
Word-grub, maggot (Latin, Endymia fatalis)
Parasitic in common parlance, epidemic in books and
                                          poetry
Known to frequent scholarship
(Though identification disputed
Owing to variety of forms)
Treat with caution
Highly contagious

The Endymion, Habitat
Endemic in long sentences, lush surroundings
                                    preferred
Not easily detected, clings tightly
Favours promises, pledges, apologies
Statements of belief especially vulnerable
In presence of alcohol
Multiplies ten-fold
Lethal if not treated

The Endymion, Feeding
Attracted to colour and speed, a speech parts
                                    omnivore
Waits at commas and hyphens, seizes prey from below
Sucks out vital fluids, leaves word shells
(Which able to occupy unrecognised)
Forages for footnotes
And afterthoughts
Resistant to treatment

The Endymion, Breeding
Self-fertilising hermaphrodite, reproduction
                                    spontaneous
In conversational flow, no known host sex preference
But believed favours leadership culture of either

But believed favours leadership culture of either
gender
Personal anecdote a delicacy
Thrives on professions of faith
Which if passionate
Provide ideal compost

The Endymion, Propagation
Preference for massy abstractions, in which prolific
egg-layer
Long gestation period during which no obvious signs
Except speech progressively hot and fevered
Emergent grubs voracious feeders
Destroy meaning overnight
Only guaranteed antidote
Silence

Jan Farquharson
GRAND CANYON

It's like heart surgery
    in the Sunday Colour Section.
We flip and say, 'Man,
    take a look!' or 'Wow!'
and set off hurriedly
    down The Bright Angel Trail.
'Hi -' we say, greeting strangers,
    'how you doing? How much
for a hole in the ground?' as if
    gags and kidding words
and things about time, our time,
    made the thing go away.
Some feed the squirrels.

Seven or eight hours later,
    returning to the top,
we stand to watch the sunset.
    A child calls out, 'It's gone,'
in a tone of real sorrow.
    We can't say a thing.
Aeons aren't ours, nor even,
    it seems, the heart.

Pamela Gillilan
PLENTY

Figs darkened in dozens along the warm wall –
sweet Brown Turkey.   And we let the grass grow.

It was shoulderhigh to our daughters,
lively with ladybirds and grasshoppers
claiming the new hayfield, homing in
to town by some mysterious instinct
shared with crowds of small delicate moths.

The children, rustling dreamily in the embrace
of the gentle forest, would disappear,
stooping to find shepherd's purse,
pink bells of bindweed, speedwell,
pimpernel, low on the parched ground.

The grass grew taller still, bleached heads
fluffed with pollen.   The whole garden rose
to the height of its rippling spread,
a cover-all that rolled and swayed,
stroked this way and that by dry winds.

A memorable indulgence, but at its end
expensive – not rhythmic scything
but a diesel scrubcutter, dragoning
blue smoke, sliced the stubble down
to fallow already seeded with twitch and fescue

foxtail, rye – and meadow-grass
and brash out-in-the-open dandelions.

David H. W. Grubb
CAGE-BIRD LOOKS AT A DISPLACED PERSON
(In response to D. J. Enright's 'Displaced Person Looks at a Cage-Bird')

I'm not going anywhere. Stick around and
do what they want you to do.
A song here, a little dance there;
a flash of the feather, a flip-over the perch and
they collapse into laughter. Seeds, water, a
safe cage; what more could you desire?
Dream? Yes; I dream. A bigger cage,
a bigger stage, a mother of all perches,
and whatever they mean by 'pulling a bird'?
Let's face it; nice little number this
when the world comes to you and there's
no vultures of hawks or hunters and
all I have to do is be seen.
As for them, as for the humans,
as for their repetitions and blobby eyes
as for the word box and the teletwizzy
thing, I think I've seen enough. They can't
be happy, poor things. They
can't settle down and assume comfort;
nests in a mess, always
squawking, mostly out of their trees.

Bill Headdon
LOCATING A CORNISH WRECK

By dead reckoning, through the lanes,
eighteen land miles from the coast;
we get a fix on marks, church lined up

with the top of Werrington,
our faulty sonar of recovered memory.
We spot the bubbles from its twin stacks

through its giveaway boil,   *
main part still lying on its side,
the dispersed outline

on the valley floor below the tree line,
its shippen and barns
in their depth of thirty years.

Then the cider orchard –
still dropping its fruit –
red as lambing; where owls took us

from our edge,
through the shelving darkness
Ten acre's sickly joint of hay, fallow,

where we came down with cousins
like corn Billies through the hills.
Survivors of a holed family

set off in their lifeboat,
swung out for the wake
of their pip-squeak years,

decks of meadows awash,
the stern of a house
about to go under,

waves of the same clouds
breaking on their infant sea,
where others must hear it break.

* *'boil' the surface disturbance caused by a wreck.*

Christopher Hedley-Dent
BUZZARDS

I saw one of their kind once
almost casually,
tethered to a perch, neutralised,
but felt as the head swivelled
side on,
the burning spot of an eye
dilate and snap tight
like a shutter,
as if I were something,
downloaded for reference.

Around here,
you sometimes come across them
mounted on tops
of telegraph poles,
their scraggy feathers
furled like an old umbrella,
shut off, just biding their time,

at others, as if caught
in a perfect long shot,
you can see the casual grace
of their wing-beat
while they indolently
trawl a field for prey,

but nothing prepares
for the upsweep of wings
surfing a hedge row,
the freeze-framed vastness
in the windscreen
and the flash point recognition
that one's just played you,
locked cunningly
into its line of sight.

Diana Hendry
THE REAL AND UNREAL SCOT

The invisible man
Who parks his car
Outside my house every night
Is a Real Scot.
It says so on his windscreen
And I believe it.
Often I lie in bed at night
Imagining what a Real Scot
Looks like.

His eyebrows are heavy
With generations.
His jaw is cleft
From the Stone of Scone.
Porridge and oatcakes
Is his complexion.
His balls are the size
Of Safeway haggis.
His hair is heather.
His kilt is tartan Swagger.
His bagpipes Wind and Lament.
His legs could leap the Cuillins,
Take Princes' Street in a single stride.

So huge is he
He'd have to fold himself in five
To squeeze inside
His grubby wee Metro.

Meanwhile
I've grown a tender spot
For the wry and subtle
Unreal Scot.

CHILD OF DOCTOR SPOCK

That *spur of the moment* thing.
Like jumping off the train at Mainz
because he liked the song she was singing.
Sailor, stop your rolling.
Only it was in German. *Seemann.*

Not for him the straight floorwalker lines
of his parents. Like a bishop or rook
on a chessboard. Sex, booze, cigarettes, spliffs,
he'd broken the rules and got away with it.
You could phrenologise the Sixties on his skull:
kibbutz in Israel, Marrakesh, Amsterdam.

An atmosphere of earnest self-improvement.
And then what was that *collective?*
A *murder* of white-coated consultants
who present him with a chamber of bullet points,
Russian roulette. Trust him to draw
the loaded one: *melanoma.*

Outside, he twirls a cigarette
in the corner of his mouth like a baton.
This wasn't how it was meant to be.
What was the proverb about white silver drawing
black lines?
He feels drawn to the darkening tracks
without the option of pulling back.

David Howard
THE GUITARIST'S FRET HAND

I am the silent partner:
unsinging, unsung
but never sleeping,

dancer,
braced and stretched
in four-way splits,
turning on a point
and leaping in time
to set waves and ripples,

mime artist,
lying prone-still
by a fret,
like a railway suicide,
becoming slow spider
and slower crab,
switching to bird
to fly and touch down quickly,

climber,
to move but stay grounded,
the one up the ladder
doing all the work,
abseiling silently down.

There is a face in the spotlight –
a close watching moon –
brow showing its own taut strings,
willing that I land lightly
and well.

Sue Hubbard
COOKING FISH

Quick as a flash –
under the ventricle fins –
a steel blade piercing wet flesh
mottled as muddied pebbles,
he scrapes out a dark trail
of guts, a mauve heart
like hidden secrets beneath
a twist of clear water
from the cold tap.

Pink flesh pale as the hidden
skin of his groin. Row
of tiny dragon teeth, milk-
white eye, a filmy moon
in the beak of a head, body
curved to the hump of the bridge
where a Chinaman hurries home
among willows of blue –
smell of dark reeds and ponds.

A meal *á deux.*
She poaches it slowly,
stuffs along the spine
with fine feathers of dill,
black pellets of peppercorn,
mushrooms, slivers of garlic sliced
thin as the aorta of her heart
that hisses and hisses
he loves, he loves me not.

Mimi Khalvati
LIFE IN ART

With the simplicity of frost,
the muddy depths of dream
you can't recall and yet – lost
as they are, they gleam

with the clarity of snowflakes
melting under an eye,
an ambiguity that wakes
to rain's late lullaby

with words as small as pronouns you
or I could take as ours,
a big heart and an old one, new
only in its scars

the way a thistle's colour draws
a thumb along its brush
and tells you it's not spiny wars
but softness that can crush

the way in lonely spots breath rises
like white manes in the mist
and lovers look for no surprises
on lips so often kissed

with these and other ways in mind
I might seduce a verse
to wake to, speak with, touch and find
that poetry's no worse

for frost and mud, snow and rain,
the languages of war,
of love that fears to hear again
abuse it's heard before

I might renew acquaintance, mend
walls I never breached
or breach them now and not pretend
I practised what I preached.

I might forget my small concerns,
leaning against the jamb,
watching the world go by that turns
me into what I am.

And as for larger griefs – well, they
are the dumb stones in my heart.
They will not speak nor I betray
life in art.

Karen Kuehne
BUILDING THE HOUSE

The sound of saws, electric, chain or hand held
cut across the smell of wood. Two-by-fours arrived
for the frame, plywood over concrete,
wide pine for the floors.

My body built itself at the same
stop-start speed. The day the windows came
I bought my first bra. Before the decks were done
Patrick next door had asked me to the dance.
His hand was sweaty, but steady
and I held it all evening long.

Father cut the wood, wielded the plumb line
and drove in nails with hands shaking
from nights of whiskey. Sometimes, a few drinks in,
he'd go back after dark to take a look,
the shell transforming,
the shape suddenly solid and strong.

V. G. Lee
BLUE MOON

Poppa played blue grass;
popped ampules of amyl nitrite,
two in each nostril – high days
and holidays as early as in the fifties.
Thought he was John Lee Hooker
setting out back on a wind cracked chair
waiting for a man in a sedan
to arrive with the money.
"Smokestack Lightnin'", "Spoonful",
you name it – he played it.

Day he died, Ma took his old burnoose
off the back door nail, not one tear she cried
as she wrapped up his acoustic guitar.
Took off her apron, fussed her hair,
slipped into Pa's blue suede shoes and shuffled
down the dirt track to where we'd dug out a ditch,
six by two in the shade of the big blue gum.
She said (and not for the first time),
"I loved him and he loved me but it broke
that music man's heart to see the kids
I bore him become blue collar workers".

As if on cue the skies opened,
tipped out a torrent of water
like we hadn't seen since seventy three,
when Tania and Marvin got wed
and we'd fried up monkfish and horse mackerel
served with a blue cheese dressing.
Pa's suede shoes were ruined, Ma tossed them
down in the grave, where they nestled
next to the womanly shape of his old guitar.

Reverend said a very few words,
"the grass withers, the flower falls",

46

we *"Amen'd"* to that and went indoors,
split a few beers, played Pa's Howlin' Wolf records.
Ma stayed out on the porch wailing that the moon
wasn't as blue as her heart, but in the morning
her tears had dried and the sun shone.
We went back to our jobs in the tanning factory,
leaving her to chop up Pa's wind cracked chair –
maybe for firewood, maybe a cross.

CHINESE BOXES

As I pause to take a snap, the red frame
of an opening draws my eye inside
telescoped rooms: stone-flagged dark, a door,
bright squares of glass, a yard, a space
with a stove. I almost expect to see
myself reflected ever smaller in each.

The very old sit outside in the sun, each
in a blue cotton suit; as they pose in the frame
of my camera, smiling, pleased, I see
how distant they look, how diminished inside
this box. I want words to span the space
but my tongue's stuck, my mouth a closed door.

A sudden scent of lilies-of-the-valley as the door
of the Beijing Metro seals us in - each
in a closed box, a dark honeycombed space -
and a lost garden brims in freeze-frame.
Along a quiet hutong, an old man inside
a house turned inside out: he stares, but we see

what he, by the window, doesn't seem to see,
his courtyard's turned to dust and his open door
now opens on nothing; what happens, happens inside
his grey brick box. Dolls' houses, each
left carelessly, broken toys in a frame.
And after it's tidied up, the empty space

will be filled with mirrored boxes in the space
of a wink, so that it's hard not to see
those high card-houses in their airy frame
squashed with the palm of the hand: one push at the
                                                    door
as they'd slide down flat. But in Chinese gardens,
                                                    each

outdoor room is precise, as if one inside

another, opened out; the windows inside
impose their latticed patterns onto space,
an arching branch or a weathered rock in each.
A kingfisher, almost too quick to see,
unravels his blue thread; through a door
plum blossom's arranged in its frame.

Inside each Chinese box, a scene in a frame:
I scan my photos, look through the half-open door
for what's at the centre, almost too small to see.

Mary Maher
DECKCHAIR

All summer it embodies
your shape

but you have no arms,
no wings

to hold you in this chair.
No cover

of dyed roses, buttoned
hide.

The candy stripes give,
dip

like a rainbow's other half
but there is no shelter

from the adorable horizon.
So adore it.

The tide is racing. Racing
to the castle.

There is salt, a shift, promenade,
the pier,

the simplest of frames.
Angles

suspend the comfort of a curve
blown

from the edge of sunshine.
A break

before winter when there'll be
waiting,

waiting with something
to wait for

in a mere oblong,
flat-packed,

like a letter which lies there
folded,

wanting to be opened
wanting.

Marion Mathieu
THE IMMORTALS

Exhausted by month-long symphonies,
great twisting novels and million-piece jigsaw puzzles
showing only the sky,
I shut out your warnings and slept.

You sponged me clean each morning,
washed and softened my sheets,
called in teams of psychiatrists and carpenters
as I grew.

Windows sprouted gangplanks for my arms and legs,
a mattress-lined veranda cushioned my mighty head.

You nestled in my ear, shouted out bits
you thought I'd like from the newspapers,
tattooed the history of our relationship
on my rapidly expanding skin.

I awoke refreshed, flattened your beauty with a slap,
plucked a tiny, ink-stained needle from my fingertip.

Flicking roof tiles from the pyjamas
you had crazy quilted your curtains to construct,
I plunged my head through the clouds,
gulped in two lungfuls of high, thin air,

stretched to my full height for one precious, dizzying
                                                    moment
and stood face to face with the sun.

Blind, burned, and gasping,
I toppled back into the atmosphere,
to voices and music too soft for me to hear
and your squashed, doll-sized love.

Denise McSheehy
AN OCCASION FOR BEING HUMAN

(after Three Studies for Figures at the Base of a Crucifixion
by Francis Bacon)

The necks have it –
and the open mouths,
the poor dear teeth

the reaching
the terrible crouch of fear

Such plain canvasses
colour of an angry sky,
a wound

and no going back – we're all there
at the foot of something
on our knees

Magdalen moving without arms
without hands

now a soft bolt of body,
little mother veiling her eyes

the lover
caught in his arched
rictus

How they weigh – maimed
lumpish

the loop of sweet line
reeling you in

to your own heart,
to the pattern of rib
printing skin

as poised
dancers, they keep balance
hold

Paul Mills
THE LAKE

Now it's night you wait in the reeds
with your bit of white floating crust among swirls,
tremors, lips, the seething
of invisible fins, the surface you are reading –
a primer without rules, except you know them,
only you know them.

From before the sun rose
to after it set we've been here
and you've hardly noticed clouds flying past,
or a plan high up in the heat somersaulting.
All your flow and somersault is with a line.

I watch your calm profile among the reeds,
fifteen, slim as a reed but growing, growing
invisibly, everything irrelevant but your fishing,
your day, the silence of your performance,
a dancer who stands still and is simply alert.

Between you and your bronze gold god, nothing
                                    distracts.
The perfect metal cast
of the thing you've imagined,
from sightreading to the delivered finish,
appears like one dreamed sleepwalking act.
You are in it even after we leave and are talking
                                    about it.

And the carp too are extravagant.
All day you've been listening
for these mouths,
waiting for their idiom to shift.
The cool of the set sun moves them about,

and when I'm standing by you with our net,
I'm not the one involved
with the line's weaving unnerved thinness
through which fish after fish express their weight,
rush to be free of it, to be again
an invisible fold of water.

I'm not the one. I'm just nearby,
watching with you while they exert
strengths nothing can simulate or pretend.
Nothing else has this convulsed, delicate
sudden pressure, or is a sum of the day's heat –
trees, cornfields, colours,
darkness soft as the moon that floats like bread.

Esther Morgan
LETTER BEFORE LEAVING

Fogbound forever
the troop ship wallows
in its slick of filth.
Cooped in the hold we squabble
like red-wattled turkeys
on Christmas Eve.

On deck we rub our eyes
in disbelief of land.
All around the city rumbles
like a rumour of bombers
over the coast. Someone sighs
India . . . in a mist of breath.

Nothing exists
except this ghostly wharf
the charcoal spar of the winch
its dripping hook.
Children have given up
waving to us.

On look-out tonight
I heard a ship's horn calling
from the starless firth
like a lost dinosaur.
I could see your hand
in front of my face

like the night you had to walk
ahead of our car
searching for the road.
I crawled at funeral pace
following your torch
all the way home.

Jenny Morris
THE PEEP SIGHT

He jumps up, black
jack-in-the-box,
huge, hurtling words.
She wants to see him small,
framed and distant,
a target aligned in that
tiny round eyehole.
She wants to hold him
as an image in her head,
shivering as on a pin,
unable to spring and tower.
She wants to put the lid
on him forever.
Her witchy hands grip
the enforcer as at last
he becomes trapped
in her range.
Now she has him
in her peep sight.

K. M. Payne
MY LOBSTER

Gerard de Nerval used to take a lobster
For walks in public gardens. He said it knew
The ocean depths and didn't bark or mew
Like common dogs or cats. They made a pair.

I keep a lobster because his rattling claws
Return a clack clack clack to the depressing
Clack clack clack of life: the ever-pressing
Demands of ex-wife, daughter, son-in-law,

Numbskull job and social slot. I claim
My anger is my lobster and his role
is to keep me passable sane. If he's not real
Yet he's a true crustacean all the same.

Mario Petrucci
LOOK

If these wicks were Grecian, not Safeway
candles fresh from their sixpack of mock
dynamite, and these floors mosaic rather than lino
then this look you give might have had limbs –

psychopodia, the ancients dubbed them.
Imagine. The eye flicking tongue-like round
these awkward angles of caramelised chicken-wing
through that chink in the door, into

the recess of my ear, which to your *psychopod*
would seem cavernous. Our eyes like fungi,
threading galaxies with their fine white mycelia,
making a spore of each star. Our vision

muscling in on the entire observable universe.
But we've made it small, this glance – chemical
signals along the optic omnibus, a buzz
in the brain. Soul's window, which the ruler turns

into a dark little room. There, in each cinema
of jelly, the filament of a London sunset glows
dimly. All that promise obeying straight lines.
And yet, even now, with our conversation

trained on quasars, distracted by lasers
scoring music (the CD you tilt from its rank
making the rainbow's arc come full circle)
that pencil of rays from your lips can't help

but sear its red purse on the sweet spot
of my retina – and for a moment, just that,
we combine the old and the new, look
deep into our looking, and walk there.

Brian Poole
GREAT RAILWAY JOURNEYS : HASLEMERE TO HAVANT

Near Liphook pendulous orange fruits in abundance.
Toucans roost and parrots shriek.
At Liss five gazelles spring off nimbly.
A seller of okra grins from the platform.

So winsome these native women in floral prints.
Heads wrapped in folds of silk,
Balancing trays of kola nuts and corn,
They sashay at the track-side, plump but lithe.

Petersfield a busy junction. Vultures
On corrugated roof-tops shift and eye
Knots of travellers stupefied by heat.
Sacks of ground-nuts piled in pyramids.

At Rowlands Castle nomadic tribesmen,
Huge white dewlapped cattle on the line.
A hissing of steam and brakes – a thud.
Our cow-catcher has caught two cows.

Havant. Flies settle and lift, settle and lift.
To my left the exit, to my right the train –
A man in uniform framed between.
'This ticket isn't valid for the eight fifteen.'

It's not a fine day that starts with a fine.
Haslemere to Havant is a dangerous line.

H. M. Shukman
THREAD

A button on my trousers has come loose.
Before it taps on the floor, sinks in a rug,
I find my hotel mending kit, Swiss Army scissors.
What would my grandfather think, the one I never
                                                                        knew,
the tailor, who glided out of war up a still, grey
                                                                        Thames,
saw the fog lift on the brick-black face of Wapping?
1910: hats and bulky overcoats, a threat
of rain, a reek of yeast, gulls truant overhead.

He running-stitched, hemmed, cuffed and collared his
                                                                        way
from Shelter to a Shoreditch flat. Then Soho, one
                                                                        mile north
of Savile Row, and finally a real house up Finchley
                                                                        Road.
Jews were always middle class, just not allowed to be.

I settle under my desk lamp, open the card,
unravel its tangled blue, then suck and find the eye.
His son's son. A middle class boy (he got me there)
who never sat cross-legged on a table, or wore
a thimble, or learnt chalk's code on cloth. I never
brushed ash from a distant gentleman's tweed,
or trimmed fox or bear, weightless astrakhan.

I prod and pull my double thread. A bath a week –
I wonder if he smelled. A grimy neck? An animal
breath of Polish sausage and tea with blackberry jam?
Did he shout at the kitchen table?   And what's left
                                                                        of him
in me, a softskinned man who doesn't use his hands,
who doesn't sing or dance or fast or pray, who bears
only the lost Yiddish scrawled on chest and shoulder?

My grandfather tuts and shakes his head. He taps my
                                                    point,
my final inch of thread, too short to tie a decent
                                                    knot.
Leave that to me, he says, *you've better things to do.*
His eyebrows are thicker than I thought, his breath
                                                    fainter.
His big-nailed fingers, strong as a fiddler's, undo my
                                                    work,
dive, twist and snap. His needle a dorsal glint in
                                                    water.
A quick bite: done. Thread to last a lifetime.

Dana Littlepage Smith
MILLENNIUM DREAMS

She left Bosnia for Elysian Fields
and almost made it - a bayou near New Orleans
where with a doctorate she can teach remedial English
at the Za-Za Gabor Community College
& go out occasionally for Cajun meals.

Who needs fiction?
This is America where she'll marry
a transvestite queen for her green card
then turn insomniac for a season.
Even Hell can't manufacture sleep,
though once there was the sweetness of Yugoslav
                    summers.

Come Mardi Gras she'll spend her nights
on Bourbon Street trying to forget the present
p;erfect, and all continuous tenses
in order to collect party beads.
Dressed as Christ for the parade,
she hadn't thought the crown
of thorns would make her bleed.

And when someone from the crowd screams,
"But what is truth?" She'll blush
& be surprised at the water
brimming her eyes. Explaining it's been
twelve months since the heard from her mother.

After a month of being holed up in her humid
room, her husband moved to Memphis,
she'll write the few of us she still calls
friends, "Whoever reads this, if you celebrate
Easter, I wish you peace."

She signs her name, sincerely,
scribbled by what could be a symbol
for the millennium: a stick figure
of a woman whose mouth is opened
in a careful yet unending scream.

FINDING THE RIGHT BLUE FOR THE WATERFALL

Hiroshige knew –

so solid a blue
the Victorian tight-rope walker
could have walked across
in the declining sun
without her white pole gleaming.

It's a metaphysical act,
intensifying the blue –
swallows in slow-motion,
stars perched on the overfall
without trepidation

as when Orpheus played.

FOR A FRIEND IN ORKNEY

Seas are ghosts of ancient clouds,
grey-skinned,
they trundle sky, roll its load
of emeralds and marble,
salting the moon.

In the prow of your house
you play Bach,
the small, antique piano releases
each note,
a flake of snow;

room fills with unseen shifts,
sounds breaking along
the windows,
metal so cold,
it could burn the skin on a hand.

Outside,
the blizzard is loosely-linked,
mesh so light,
it floats upward,
it is the mineral of the music;

drifts accumulating silence
above the abyss,
where cadence is most profound.

John Whitworth
DOCTOR DOUBLEGOER'S PRESCRIPTIONS

Whisky straightens out my head.
I'm as drunk as Noah.
Someone's standing by my bed
(Whisky straightens out my head)
Who is that standing by my bed?
It's Doctor Doublegoer.

Weave your gold and silver thread.
Wear your jewel lower.
Feed me fruit and feed me bread
(Then wind me, bind me, wanton threat),
For Passionfruit and Gingerbread
Suit Doctor Doublegoer.

Bite me with your hammerhead,
Squeeze me with your boa.
Both of them look underfed
(Oh bite me with your hammerhead),
Definitively underfed
Like Doctor Doublegoer.

Something nasty in the shed
Lurks behind the mower.
Harbingers of Doom and Dread
(So very nasty in the shed)
Chill the blood with Doom and Dread
Of Doctor Doublegoer.

Hide my eyes in Holyhead,
Hide my feet in Goa,
Hide my heavy heart in lead
(My holy eyes in Holyhead),
My holy heart in heavy lead
For Doctor Doublegoer.

Don't forget the things I said.
Get him on the blower.
The lot of us are Damned and Dead
(The things, the things, the things I said),
As double Damned and doornail Dead
As Doctor Doublegoer.

NOTES ON WINNERS

Greta Stoddart, born in 1966, is currently working on her first collection. Her poems have appeared in POETRY REVIEW, VERSE, THE NORTH and THE INDEPENDENT ON SUNDAY.

Sheenagh Pugh was born in 1950 and teaches Creative Writing at the University of Glamorgan. She lives in Cardiff, and her last collection, published by Seren, was *'ID'S HOSPIT'*. She was awarded the Forward Poetry Prize ('98) for the best individual poem.

John Mole was born in Taunton. His *SELECTED POEMS* (Sinclair-Stevenson*)* was published in 1955. He received the Gregory, Cholmondely and (for children's poetry) Signal awards. Forthcoming collections are *FOR THE MOMENT* (Peterloo) and *THE DUMMY'S DILEMMA* (Hodder).

Terry Pritchard has been published in Small Press Magazines. He lives in Crediton with a wife and two children who describe him as 'a renaissance hippie in carpet slippers and sad cardigan'.